# COPYRIGHT NOTICE

For more information about *99+ Speaker Success Tips, Tactics, Strategies & "Don't Forget" Actionable Items*; individual orders; bundled orders, discounts for bulk-quantity purchases; audio products; interviews; information on seminars; JV opportunities; mentoring/consulting; booking Bart Smith to speak at your next seminar, workshop or event; please contact the author through any of his websites:

# BARTSMITH.COM

**INCOME DISCLAIMER:** Every effort has been made to accurately represent the subject nature of this book and all its potential. Even though most industries are ones where a person can "write their own ticket" in terms of earning potential, there is "no guarantee" that you will earn any money using the teachings, lessons and ideas found in this book. Any examples provided are not to be interpreted as a promise or guarantee of earnings. Earning potential is entirely dependent upon the sincere effort and the effective use of what is found in this book and on your own individual effort, circumstances and more. That said, here's to your success.

# TABLE OF CONTENTS

As you can see, I essentially wrote this book in three main parts. The book is broken up into speaker success tips to implement **BEFORE**, **WHILE** and **AFTER** you speak.

After reading this book and following as many of my tips and suggestions as possible, see how your own speaker **performance**, **results** and **success** improves almost INSTANTLY! Hey, in advance, I look forward to great days ahead for you as a speaker, presenter, seminar leader and more!

# ABOUT THE AUTHOR

**B**ART SMITH is the author of 27 books on business, marketing, motivation, lethal confidence, dating and relationships, coaching, personal development, self-publishing, networking, cooking/cookbook, and *SPEAKING!* If you enjoy listening to audiobooks, Bart has recorded most of his books in audio for you to listen to as well, including this book. Listen for free at *BartSmith.com/audio*.

BART also created *SpeakerCafe.com*, a speaker directory, to help speakers showcase their speaking talents to companies and organizations who might book them for speaking engagements.

One of BART'S PASSIONS (and business pursuits) is baking the world's best chocolate chip cookies since 1988. Really, check it out at **BartsCookies.com** and **iLoveBartsCookies.com**.

# MESSAGE FROM THE AUTHOR

Hey, I'm really excited you picked up my book. Having a desire to speak usually comes with a host of challenges most speakers encounter on their way up the speaker mountain of success. Inside this book, I have created a list of **99+ SPEAKER SUCCESS TACTICS** to ensure that climb to the top will be a smooth and successful one.

That said, I've accumulated these speaker tips, tactics and actionable items every speaker should be aware of to help improve their chances at becoming a really great speaker. Whether you speak for free or get paid to speak, I know these speaker success insights will help you become a better, more polished speaker even after a single reading of this book.

And then, to become a great speaker, by putting in the time, practice, finding opportunities to put your speaking talents to the test, along with your desire to keep improving with every presentation you give, speaker success is absolutely right around the corner. Just imagine now, how much farther/faster you'll go with your speaking talents once you become aware of the 99+ speaker success tips to implement!

Well, here's to your hard work, dedication and dreams of becoming a show-stopping speaker! I can see you on stage now rocking the audience with your well-crafted, well-rehearsed and well-planned presentation.

As they say in show business, "knock em dead, kid." I hope you blow them all away with your awesome speaking performances. Show 'em what you've got!!!

# FORWARD BY

## LEISA REID

### PROFESSIONAL SPEAKER AND FOUNDER OF

GetSpeakingGigsNow.com

iSpeakerNetwork.com

**W**ith 500+ booked/delivered speaking engagements and founder of *GetSpeakingGigsNow.com* and *iSpeakerNetwork.com*, I was more than happy to read through Bart's **99+ SPEAKER SUCCESS TACTICS**! Wow, what an amazing "don't forget to do" type of actionable items for all speakers! After reading through them, I can attest that everything Bart mentioned is what every speaker show learn and do at some point in their speaking career. He practically leaves no "speaker tip" stone unturned.

What's more, I like what Bart mentioned about getting a speaker mentor to help you take your speaking skills to the next level. As someone who mentors business professionals and entrepreneurs who want to make an impact and ultimately attract their ideal clients through speaking, I'd say Bart's book is required reading. As a speaker myself, and someone who's worked with hundreds of speakers, we can all benefit from Bart's amazing list of **99+SPEAKER SUCCESS TACTICS**. As speakers, we can never stop learning to improve our speaker craft. Thanks, Bart, for sharing them with us!

*Leisa Reid*

# PART 1

# BEFORE
# YOU SPEAK

Here are a number of speaker success tips, tactics and actionable items you should remember to implement **BEFORE** you speak.

1. **Prepare and rehearse your speech several times.** Draft an outline for it, time it, and be sure you can get through all your points in a designated period of time. With an outline, you're better able to stay on point and not drift off on tangents which then waste even more time. You might also record your speech before you give it, perhaps on your phone and then listen to it over and over if that helps you to memorize it.

2. **Practice, practice, practice and even get feedback from someone near you** who can help you fix, adjust, tweak, add or drop something from your speech.

3. **Rehearse and memorize your FIRST and LAST lines.** They're what people remember the most. If you can come up with great opening and closing statements or two, wow, your speech will be a big hit with your audience and easy for you to open and close.

4. **When drafting your speech and creating your outline, remember that "LESS IS MORE."** The structure of your talk should go like this: (#1) your opening statement(s), (#2) 3-5 main points, (#3) 3-5 stories or case studies that support your main points, (#4) some audience participation, and (#5) closing statements summarizing what you spoke about along with any type of motivational statements to the audience to take action on what they learned. That's it, minus a few tweaks and adjustments to finalize your speech. With a strong opening, mention your first main point, and then tell your story. Transition to your second main point, then give another example, and so forth. Your stories bridge everything together. With a strong opening and motivating close, your speech should be a rocking success!

5. **Keep your talk/outline and talking points short and concise.** Ask yourself, "Does my audience really need to know this?" If you

can reference something (in more detail) on your website or in the handout you gave your audience, then keep your spoken word crisp, clean, short and to-the-point to address the ever-shrinking attention span of your listeners.

6. **Create three checklists that will help you: (1) remember what to bring to the speaking event, (2) what to do at the speaking event and (3) what to remember to do or take home with you after the speaking event is over.** Checklists help us stay organized amidst all the chaos, fun and excitement going on with your speaking gig. "Let's see, I'm leaving so let's make sure I have everything ... [ ] Check ... [ ]  Got it ... [ ] Where's my extension cord? Don't want to forget that."

7. **Prepare any handouts, flyers, order forms, etc. days before the event and not the night before the event.** It takes time to create them, proof them, get copies at your local copy store, etc. Don't waste precious time the day before designing forms and making copies when you could be reviewing your speech and relaxing.

8. **Order books and other inventory you'd like to sell at the event weeks ahead of your speech so you have inventory in hand to bring and sell!** Don't give a speech and not bring product to sell at the back of the room. What a wasted opportunity. Even if you don't sell anything, at least you were prepared.

9. **Test and charge your PayPal or Stripe credit card readers for your phone and make sure you know how to charge a credit card.** Don't be breaking out the manual or reading Help files on your phone while people are waiting to buy your book, etc. Also, if you don't have a credit card reader, order this now so you have it for your next speaking gig. People will buy what you have to sell with credit cards. Be ready.

10. **Test your website. Make sure it's up and running.** If you tell people to go to it, make sure it's working properly along with the shopping cart and opt-in forms so people can make use of them

and not run into a 404 page not found or other errors.

11. **Pack up your stuff and place it in the car the night before or on a table to quickly grab it on your way out the door to give your speech.** You've got time the night before to do this kind of prep. Take advantage of it.

12. **Have a number of different outfits dry cleaned and available to pick and choose.** Different audiences require/allow for different wardrobe appearances. Plus, you might try something on the day of the speech and not like it.

13. **Research who your audience is, the company you're speaking for, problems your audience faces** or some recent statistics to personalize your opening speech, etc.

14. **Get specific directions to the location where you'll speak. If you're driving to the event, have an alternative route in case of traffic delays.** If traffic is usually high at certain times, leave an hour earlier. It's better to sit in your car in the parking lot at the event than in your car or on some freeway that might be backed up for hours due to an unforeseen accident.

15. **Become a good storyteller by experiencing life, remembering those highlights,** listening to others tell their stories and be able to retell those events and experiences in ways that leave people smiling, laughing or crying, whatever reaction you're going for.

16. **Don't overload your slides, if you plan on using them in your speech.** Keep each slide to no more than one paragraph of 3-5 sentences. When using lists, keep them to seven bullet points or less. Go over your slides several times, too. Become one with your own material. Use LARGE FONTS and as FEW WORDS AS POSSIBLE so people in the back can see your slides.

17. **Do you have a speaker one-sheet created to help you get**

**speaker gigs?** If not, design one. Even if you have one, check out my special report on how to create the perfect speaker one-sheet at *MyTrainingCenter.com/speaker-one-sheet*.

18. **Not speaking enough? Network and befriend other speakers.** Speak at their events, share event leads with them and encourage them to share theirs with you. If speakers have too many offerings, maybe they can pass them on to you and vice versa.

19. **Leave an extra 60 minutes earlier and arrive early to relax prior to your speech.** You can always rest up in the car going over your notes and speech. Plus, you may need time to find the room you're speaking in or you might need time to set up your booth/table, equipment, or find a safe place for your belongings.

20. **Where's your book? Don't have one ... yet?** Well, let's write one because they make for great sales in the back of the room, and it can be the basis for a speech, class, workshop to get you interviewed for more exposure! Plus, books establish you as an authority on what you're speaking about. If you do have a book, did you record it? That can be sold in the back of the room for higher profit margins. Sell your book for $20 and add $10 or more for the audio version bundle and you just made a healthy sale to one person.

21. **Spend time at the event before your speech meeting people and asking them to share their questions about the topic you'll be speaking on.** You can use those questions in your speech. "Earlier, I was talking to someone who asked me (x). What a great question ..."

22. **If you don't have time after the event to take pictures**, be sure to take a few of the building, building/event sign, with the host and audience members, coordinators, the room, the stage, other booths/tables, etc.

23. **Watch other great speakers present their topics.** Do this regularly. While you wait for your next speaking gig, check out

YouTube.com frequently to listen and watch other speakers. Learn from them, watch them, observe small things they say or do that make their performance stand out.

24. **Test any equipment you might be using the night before or before you go on stage.** This includes microphones (bring your own if you have a special one), overhead projector and hookup, laptop connection, WiFi, special lighting you might need, etc.

25. **Charge your cell phone to 100% and bring your wall charger or pocket battery charger.** If you're going to use it for directions, photos, record video and audio, you need to be sure your phone isn't at 20% power by the time you need it most before, during or after your speech.

26. **Plan how you might time your speech.** Look for a clock, ask a member of the audience to hold up their hand at a certain point, ask the host to do the same. Do this to ensure you get your speech in, make all your points and don't run over or out of time.

27. **Have cash on hand for change** when selling merchandise, at least a $100 worth of $5s, $10s, $20s.

28. **If you decide to use a laser pointer**, consider green or blue and not red. Keep extra batteries on hand.

29. **Come up with a prize or a number of giveaways** as a way to collect business cards or a sign-up sheet for names, eMail addresses and phone numbers. I think phone numbers are easier to read and sometimes people prefer texting vs. eMailing.

30. **Get a good night's sleep before the event.** Eat light (or not at all) hours before you speak so you don't get on stage feeling full and bloated, burping with every breath, etc. Appear light on your feet and super energetic. Be mindful not to drink alcohol as well before your speech thinking it will ease your anxiety. Save eating and drinking for after your speech.

31. **Transportation preparation including filling up your car with gas the day before** your speaking gig, is imperative if you are driving. If you plan to use Uber or Lyft, make sure those apps are installed, functioning and funded so you're not fumbling last minute trying to call for a ride and pay for it.

32. **Watch other speakers at the event you're speaking at before you get up to speak.** What are they talking about that you can use to help bridge their speeches with yours? "One of the other speakers today mentioned (x) and I'd like to elaborate on that a little bit ..." Plus, you'll know what not to talk about if they already discussed topic-x or what to talk about because they didn't cover something, or very well, and you have more information.

33. **Walk around the event, if you're speaking at an event with other speakers, and look at the booths/tables they've set up.** What do they have on their tables? What are they selling, offering or giving away? Take notes of what you like and don't like so your booth/table rocks the next time around!

34. **Not committing enough time daily/weekly to score more speaking gigs.** Got no gigs? This is the best time to score some ... before you speak! Don't wait for them to come to you, unless your phone is ringing off the hook with new speaking leads.

35. **If you can't find speaking gigs, setup your own.** Conduct your own seminar, class, workshop, etc. together to keep your speaking talents sharp and fresh on your mind. Use those events to convince others to book you for their events. Take pictures; gather audience video testimonials, etc.

36. **Your first few statements can really set the tone** for your entire speech, so plan this out well. Once you're in the zone, on a roll, etc.

37. **Don't be nervous. Have fun with this. SMILE and enjoy yourself.** If you can make people laugh, and not with jokes, but just a warm and natural sense of humor, your speech can

actually make people feel really good about your content. This is your chance to connect with people you don't know.

38. **Take care of yourself, health wise.** Eat well, sleep well, work out, look your best, sound vibrant, energetic and on fire when you give every speech!

39. **Work with a speaker mentor or trainer** to help you improve your speaker performance.

40. **Work on your speaker materials, speaker kit, speaker reel, web page** about the services/topics you can speak on. No speaking gigs yet? Work smart on your material to get them.

41. **If you don't have any video of you speaking,** fake it 'til you make it! That is, pick one or more of your best speeches and film yourself speaking for 3-10 minutes per speech. Upload those videos to your website for show 'n' tells. When you have the opportunity to film yourself speaking before a real audience, take advantage in that moment to video record yourself. Until then, any video of you showing what you look like, how you sound and what you have to say can go a long way.

42. **Be mindful that you don't fill your presentation with too many technical words,** jargon or phrases. Keep it simple. Avoid creating presentations that are complicated and have too much detailed information to absorb in one sitting.

43. **Include examples your audience can relate to** in your presentation.

44. **Include visuals, photos and video in your presentations.** Don't make them overly text/list-based.

45. **Don't be nervous. The more you practice and rehearse the more comfortable you'll feel.** Nervousness is a sign that you might not be prepared. So, prepare and watch your anxiety go away. Plus, in the back of this book I have my *Presentation*

*Nervousness Be Gone* report for you.

46. **Visit the room you're going to speak in.** If you have access to the room where you'll be speaking, check out every detail. Look around for wall chargers (do you need your own extension cord), test that WiFi works well (good signal; not weak), and check the lighting. Do you like how the seats are arranged, make any audio/video equipment change/arrangements and practice standing in the exact spot where you'll be making your presentation.

47. **Ask if your speech will be recorded, if so, can you get a copy?** If not, can YOU record it? Whether you record the video portion or the audio, record something! You can use this recording later in a future speaker reel you might make or just for show on your website or social media. If the host or facility can't or won't record you, record yourself with your phone. Stick a lavalier microphone into your phone, slip your phone in your back pocket (or so), and record your talk. You can use that recording for so many purposes: self-evaluation, for sale after your speech, samples on your website ... you name it!

48. **Ask someone in the audience to film you (and take pictures of you) for a few minutes with your phone.** Show them how. Do a quick test video recording session, and then tell them when to start filming. Preferably, be sure to film the start of your speech, some in the middle and the end. IF you can't do that, at least film yourself giving your introduction. It's authentic, you're there, you're fired up, so record at least the first few minutes at the start of your speech in that environment.

49. **Take 5 minutes or so before your speech and GET IN THE ZONE!** Get psyched and amped up! You're about to rock your audience and make an impact on their lives. Be prepared and feel good about that!

■  ■  ■

# PART 2

## IMPLEMENT THESE SPEAKER SUCCESS TIPS

# WHILE
## YOU ARE
## SPEAKING

Here are a number of speaker success tips, tactics and actionable items you should remember to implement **WHILE** you speak.

1. **Don't start out with a boring statement.** Instead, what is the most exciting thing you can say to get your audience going?

2. **Do not say that you are nervous, sorry, unprepared, reluctant, unqualified or not good at public speaking.** Admit NOTHING! Never apologise. Just get up there and speak! Begin with the powerful opening statement you practiced. With every speech you give, all those issues will hopefully go away quickly! *"Do it and get through it,"* I say. If you're nervous, don't let your feelings of uneasiness take away from your presentation.

3. **Before you get into your presentation, tell your audience exactly what they'll learn.** Set them up for success by saying, "In my talk today, you're going to learn _____ so that you can _____." Let them know whether (or when) you'll stop for breaks, if you'll be accepting questions during your presentation, etc. Offering these presentation "signposts" up front gives your audience a clear idea of what to expect, so they too can relax and focus on your amazing presentation coming up.

4. **Start your speech off with something the audience can connect with or relate to,** whether it's a statistic, a story or other mention.

5. **Don't attempt to make a ton of key points.** Make 1-2 key points for a short talk (i.e., 15 minutes) and 4-5 points for a 30-minute talk, etc.

6. **Start your speech off with audience participation if it makes sense!** *"So, the topic I'm going to talk about today is ____. Would anyone like to share their experiences with ____ before we get going?"* Doing this gets the audience tuned up, tuned in, awake and enthusiastically engaged because they actually have a say in the topic you're presenting on. They're just not going to sit there for an hour (or more). They can actually speak and voice what's on their minds. That can be fuel for your speech if you didn't know that!

7. **PERFORM, ACT, ENTERTAIN ... just don't teach, speak and train.** You're an entertainer first, while you deliver your material. At the end of your presentation, you want people to look forward to meeting you in person and not walking out having just heard a boring speech.

8. **Make your audience laugh.** Laughter is a great way to relax both you and your audience. A warm, natural sense of humor is all you need. One simple statement can often times win your audiences in your favor before you get into the meat of your topic. Drop brief, funny statements throughout your talk and you'll have folks smiling throughout your presentation.

9. **Don't bury yourself in your notes.** Use them for reference, but look up quickly and face your audience 90% of the time.

10. **DON'T TALK FAST!** Pause between thoughts/ideas. Don't forget to breathe. Speak clearly taking small breaks between words and points you want to make. Allow people time to digest what you're saying. Don't fire

hose them to death. Speakers who speak fast are either super nervous, don't believe what they're saying is true and valid or think they need to convince you with a lot of information in the hope that you'll believe and buy from them. HOGWASH! People can make up their own minds about what you have to sell or tell. Speak in a comfortable manner that actually draws them into you and doesn't push them away from you. Besides, if people are taking notes, talking too fast won't allow them to truly absorb what you're talking about.

11. **Make individual eye contact with your audience and not just one individual throughout your presentation.** Look into the eyes of everyone in your audience individually. Give them that personal attention. Make them feel special, as if you're talking directly to them, and make them smile. Don't let your eyes dart around the room without ever pausing to acknowledge the recipients of your message. A lack of eye contact can mean several things, such as, insincerity, dishonesty, nervousness, arrogance, deception, disengagement, and disinterest.

12. **Ask the people in the far back of the room if they can hear you** clearly and early on in your presentation.

13. **Before you start your speech or sometime during your presentation, allow people to stand up and stretch a bit.** Maybe they've been sitting there for a long time and need to move about to avoid falling asleep. Get them up to keep both of you invigorated and paying attention!

14. **Walk around the stage, walk towards / into the audience, become one with them.** Just don't stand behind

the podium. Move around. People like that. It helps THEM to stay alert and listening by keeping their heads and eyes moving as you move about.

15. **Watch out for distracting mannerisms** such as robotic pacing, turning your back to the audience too much, using/waving your hands too much, adjusting your hair or clothing too much, holding on to the lectern too long, fidgeting with props, pointer or a pen, touching your face too often, licking your lips, placing your arms behind your back for too long (while you walk too), putting your hands in your pockets (for too long). Don't fiddle with things in your pocket like keys (empty your pockets when you go on stage) or bob your head too much, etc. If you can, record your presentations, watch them to see if you do anything that you find annoying and stop it!

16. **Watch your "ums", "wells," and "uhs"**, uh, seriously! Instead of saying those words, just PAUSE for a second, while you gather your next talking point. Bite your tongue so you don't say those words and proceed to the next part of your speech. Think, speak, pause ... repeat.

17. **Lean into your audience.** Just don't stand there or slouch or lean back. Lean forward from time to time as if you're going to jump out into your audience and crowd surf them like a rock star lead singer might do.

18. **Come up with exercises the audience can participate in** to better learn what it is you're speaking to them about.

19. **Avoid data dumping and fire hosing your audience to death with too much information.** The average adult has

only 15-25 minutes of attention span bandwidth before they need a break or a change of topic.

20. **Make a number of personal notes to yourself while you speak** of things to repeat, not to repeat, to say again (because it went over well), or not to say or do.

21. **Use props and other lifelike examples if possible to help express what's in your speech.** Just don't tell them, show them! Have samples you can hand out to the audience to pass around among audience members.

22. **Vary your cadence, tone and pitch** so people aren't put to sleep (or annoyed) with the constant flow of words coming out of your mouth. Avoid sounding monotone as well!

23. **Hand out mini-surveys, handouts, etc. during your speech so people can engage their brain while you speak.** Maybe they can listen while writing stuff down on a specific handout you gave them. "I'm passing out this little form I want you to use to write down the answers to these 3 very important questions." You stir up the audience when you hand stuff out and they like to be more involved in your speech than just sitting there listening. Engage their eyes, hands and brain at the same time.

24. **Ask an audience member or two to share what they've learned so far in your speech (before it's over).** Get a few to share. "So far, what is one thing that stands out from what I've said about topic-x? Anyone care to share?" This reinforces the value your speech has on people in the audience. "Wow, I'm not the only one getting something

out of this speech I'm hearing today." Don't give your speech and not find out what people thought about it. Stop in the middle and find out and then keep going. This prepares people to give you their testimonial later after the speech.

25. **Mention a few times throughout your presentation that you have a giveaway** and that folks should give you their business card or fill out their name + email + phone number on your name sheet on a clipboard. Just pass around the clipboard or bowl to the audience while you continue your speech. If it's a really large audience, just have people meet you in the back of the room after your speech to give you their card or name and email.

26. **Stop your speech at certain points to ask your audience if they have any questions.** Check in with them. "Does anyone have any questions before I move on to the next topic?" At least ask and make notes of them even if you don't have time to answer them at that moment. You can quickly run through questions at the end of your presentation.

27. **Don't embarrass anyone in the audience** by calling someone out to share their story only for you to say something negative or demeaning. We've heard speakers do this. Don't let that be you. Be kind, respectful and uplifting.

28. **Don't just sell, pitch and talk about what it is you're selling.** Educate, inform, entertain, train and give your audience real value. Remember, 80% training and education; 10% answering questions; and 10% selling,

making your offer and closing folks on what you have to sell -- provided you're selling something. Otherwise, it's a simple, "Thank you for having me. I hope you learned something. I'll be in the back of the room if you have questions or would like to buy my book, etc."

29. **Repeat something you said if it bears repeating.** There's value in repeating content a second time to impress, make a point or highlight. It's a good idea.

30. **Look around the room as you speak. Is anyone nodding off, falling asleep, yawning, or looking bored?** Maybe it's a great time to change your speaking tone, volume and/or say something aloud and exciting! Perhaps, get people to stand up again, shake it out and prepare them for the next phase of your speech.

31. **Go over all the main points you spoke on.** Make sure everyone understands and absorbs what you talked about to reinforce the learning. Ask if anyone has any questions.

32. **At the end, offer to visit with people after your talk** and that you're available for questions, etc.

33. **Mention, "If you like this presentation and you'd like me to give this talk to your audience,** whether it's live in person, over the phone via teleseminar or online via webinar, I'd be glad to do that. Talk to me afterwards and we'll discuss how to make that happen."

34. **Don't answer unplanned questions from the audience only to be distracted and off on a tangent thereby extending the duration of your speech** to run out of time

and can't finish on that high note you were planning to. Save such questions for after your presentation when you can spend more time in the back of the room answering questions. It shows that you are approachable, generally interested in their feedback, and that's a plus.

35. **FINISH ON TIME!** Don't get cut off by the bell and don't rush your presentation so you finish before your time is up, either.

36. **END STRONG!** Wrap up your key points, emphasizing points you think folks should remember most and take home with them. End on a high note by leaving them with a quote, call-to-action step, homework to do, etc.

■  ■  ■

# PART 3

# AFTER
# YOU SPEAK

Here are a number of speaker success tips, tactics and actionable items you should remember to implement **AFTER** you speak.

1. **Take pictures with your audience**, the host, the room, people standing up networking, etc.

2. **Get video testimonials from people who saw you speak.** Get at least 1-3 minimum.

3. **Hand out a speaker feedback form to your audience to get just that … feedback on how you did,** content of your speech, and what you can do to improve. Have a check box on the form that gives you permission to use people's feedback in the form of a testimonial.

4. **Stay as long as you can after your speech to answer questions, network, take pictures, even help the host clean up.** You'll score points and get asked back assuredly. PLUS this is an opportunity to ask for a testimonial about your speech. "The speaker was wonderful. The audience loved him/her and they were especially nice to our staff and …" You can imagine.

5. **Stick around and watch other speakers that follow your presentation.** What can you learn? Any ideas, tips, things to say/not say? Make note of any mistakes they make!

6. **Thank everyone who invited you to speak, the host, other speakers, the staff,** sound/stage crew, audience members, security … get pictures with everyone if possible.

7. **Get the contact information from those you just met** who you'd like to stay in contact with.

8. **Double check that you have everything before you depart.** This sounds like a given, but how easily we can forget if we're in a new and strange place, having talked to a roomful of strangers for hours, excited, etc. Look around, check your bag/purse, your wallet, phone, money you made selling your books (etc.), wall charger, etc. You may never return to that location and may never get back the item you forgot, especially if it's valuable. Trust no one, suspect everyone. It takes one minute to check to see that you have everything before you leave the building.

9. **Say goodbye, personally, to as many people that you can on your way out the door.** Go out of your way to do so. You'll be the last person, hopefully, those people see before they leave the event. It'll be great to be on their minds and not someone else, right?

10. **Review your speech, in audio or video format or from memory.** How'd you do? Get feedback from others and make improvements before the next one. Make a number of personal notes to yourself after you speak of things to repeat / not to repeat, to bring / not to bring, or to do or not so your next speaking gig is an over-the-top successful compared to your last performance.

11. **Replenish any inventory or handouts** so you have them in time for the next speech.

12. **Follow up with the person who invited you to speak** at their event, company or location. Find out if they have any feedback for you. Share what you heard others say about your presentation. Encourage them to invite you back when they need another guest speaker.

13. **Don't be hard on yourself** if you think you didn't do as well as you'd like to. Every speech is a learning experience.

14. **Post photos and video of your recent speaking engagement on social media** to let people know you're out there and available to speak at their events.

15. **Update your speaker one-sheet** with new photos, testimonials, additional clients you spoke for from recent speaking engagement(s). Upload this revised speaker one-sheet to your website and you're on your way to getting more speaking gigs! Congrats!

16. **Speak as often as you can.** Don't let too much time go between speeches that you get lazy and don't pursue other speaking gigs. The more you speak, the more you can hone your speaking skills, perfect your delivery style, fine-tune your outline and the content you discuss, and so much more. The more you speak, the more gigs you'll get. It's funny how that works. To become a great speaker, keep speaking, continue to improve, and use mentors and other great speakers to refine every aspect of your presentations until one day, very soon … **YOU TOO will BECOME A WELL-KNOWN, SOUGHT-AFTER SPEAKING ROCK STAR!**

■  ■  ■

# BONUS REPORT

## PRESENTATION
## NERVOUSNESS
## *BE GONE!*

### BY
### BART SMITH

It's YOUR turn! The very second we hear someone call our name "... it's your turn - you're up!" ... is when you'd rather die than step out on stage in front of a room full of total strangers ... Right? You bet!

Do you ever experience presentation nervousness? We've all been there ... butterflies, acid churning inside our stomachs, etc. In reality, NERVOUSNESS is a lot like FIRE – it has BOTH the power to DESTROY and the ability to SERVE! Which do you CHOOSE? Don't answer that! To SERVE, of course!

Well, you're in luck! Here's how I knock my presentations out of the park! Below, I've outlined a number of PERSONAL, LOGICAL and MENTAL STEPS for you to consider, possibly implement and keep in perspective to help turn all your NERVOUS ENERGY into POSITIVE ACTION ENERGY every time you present or perform!

# HERE'S HOW YOU ELIMINATE PRESENTATION NERVOUSNESS!

1. **KNOW your SUBJECT TOO WELL!** This cannot be stressed enough! STUDY it! PREPARE it! LEARN it! BECOME it ... until your subject/topic becomes SECOND NATURE to your entire BEING!

2. **ENTERTAIN your audience** ... Turn the event/presentation/ performance into something both you and your audience will ENJOY! Consider your audience your new FAN BASE (i.e., supporting you while you're up there, rather than "it's me against them" kind of attitude.) Your audience is there to ENJOY/BENEFIT from the very information you have to

share ... just as much as you will enjoy and/or benefit from giving your presentation/performance to your audience. It's a WIN-WIN situation every time.

3. **Have PASSION for your SUBJECT/TOPIC and your AUDIENCE!** Show a little compassion. "Hey, listen up! I've something important to share with you that could help/entertain you! Now, let's get started, shall we?!?!"

4. **PRACTICE makes PERFECT every time!** SPEAK as OFTEN as you can! Lesson to learn: Imagine how great your presentation/performance would be if you've already given 1,000 presentations/performances ... Pretty good, right? Believe in yourself.

5. **WATCH and STUDY as many presenters/performers as you can.** MODEL the positive presenters/performers you like. Incorporate the little things they do with your own personal style. Also, make special note of those things that you do not like and remember not to repeat their mistakes when you give your presentation. Lesson to learn: Imagine how great your presentation/performance would be if you could observe over 1,000 presentations/performances by others of different subjects, styles and levels of profession ... Pretty good, right? Better believe it! Goal: Look at yourself as a continuous improvement project with every presentation/performance that you give or observe.

6. **THROW IT AWAY! GIVE IT YOUR BEST SHOT** and DON'T WORRY! ... If they don't get it - and you DID YOUR BEST - you DID a GREAT JOB anyway! Just GET UP THERE, GIVE IT YOUR BEST SHOT and HAVE FUN with it!

7. **ROLE PLAY** every chance you get! Again, PRACTICE makes PERFECT! Stand up and speak out loud (to an empty shower stall, rehearsal in the car, or while silently waiting in line at the grocery store. Role play every chance you get.

8. **VISUALIZE yourself on stage and loving it!** ... VISUALIZE yourself having fun with your audience. VISUALIZE successful presentations every time!

9. **VISUALIZE your audience LOVING what you have to say** and benefiting from the information/presentation you have to share with them! VISUALIZE the applause! (It's confirmation that your presentation/performance was well-received!)

10. **ENJOY the RUSSSHHH!** ... Take all that NERVOUS ENERGY and TURN IT right into ACTIVE/ACTION ENERGY in every presentation and performance going forward!

And, if that wasn't enough to make you into a rock star speaker, here are a few more tips for you when it comes to eliminating presentation nervousness:

11. **KNOW THE ROOM** ... Study it before you step on stage. Walk around the room covering the very front, back and side to side of the room. Get the "lay of the land. Then, step on stage and get a feel for where you'll be speaking from. Walk around the stage; walk from one side to another, back and forth from the front to the back. Before you know it, that stage and room will be all about you! You will be ONE with the room when you speak and making for confident, comfortable presentation. If you know where you'll be sitting, before you're called to speak, plan ahead, know

how best to access the front of the room or to reach the stage. You don't want to go down some long aisle only to find out there's no way for you to get on stage other than jumping over a table, a chair or leaping five feet in the air ... So, know the room you'll be speaking in.

12. **KNOW YOUR AUDIENCE** ... Who are you speaking to? Can you meet some of the audience members before your speech? It's always nice to speak to some of the people who will be sitting in the audience before you get up there. Knowing people in the crowd by name (because you met them) helps a lot when it comes to removing the nervousness of not knowing any one. So, meet and greet some of the folks you'll be speaking to. They'll enjoy meeting you, too, prior to going on stage. Imagine walking on stage and you've already met a handful of eager fans wanting you to succeed!

13. **NEVER APOLOGIZE FOR BEING NERVOUS** ... This is a must. NEVER admit to feeling nervous, just go on with the show. If you tell people you're nervous, they'll be nervous for you (as well) and won't enjoy your presentation as much. Besides, once you start, 99.99% of the audience won't even notice you're nervous unless ... you forget your name or what you're speaking about, which isn't going to happen because you're well-prepared; eager to get started.

14. **FOCUS ON YOUR MISSION (MESSAGE)** ... Remember you're there to speak with purpose. You're there to deliver a presentation where people will learn even more about your topic. Step up, and speak with conviction, drive and purpose as if you're on a special mission to spread your message from town to town, coast to coast, sea to shining

sea. I'm not kidding!

15. **TURN NERVOUSNESS INTO FUN, ENTHUSIASM & POSITIVE ENERGY** ... Hey, you might as well get up there and sing and dance your way through your presentation, unless, you're actually singing a real song or dancing, the point here is to have fun. Turn that nervousness into the kind of positive energy that'll make you shine. Smile, enjoy yourself, you're among friends who can't wait to hear what you have to say ... I know I would be if I were in your audience listening to you speaking. Go for it! You're an awesome speaker!

That's it! I hope this list of presentation nervousness "be gone" tips gives you the confidence you may need to make your best performance yet.

To your "SPEAKING" success,

*Bart Smith*

BART SMITH
*SpeakerCafe.com*
*ReallyCheapNames.com*
*CoachingClientForms.com*
*BartsCookbook.com*
*BartsCookies.com*

# SPEAKER SUCCESS WRAP-UP!

So, what did you learn from this book? Hopefully, you picked up a number of great inspirational tips for improving any speaking engagement, right? I hope you'll use my book as a ready reference and checklist to ensure that you know what to do before, during, and after any speech and that it inspires you to keep speaking.

Remember, the more you speak, the better speaker you become. I, too, use this book to remind myself of the many mistakes, tips, tactics and actionable items I need to think about for my own speaking performances.

In summary, with practice, repetition, regular speaking activities, trying out new material and learning from each speaking experience, you will be well on your way to becoming that rock star speaker faster than you can say, "Thank you for having me, I'm so glad to be here … now, let's get started!"

To your "SPEAKING" success,

*Bart Smith*

BART SMITH
*SpeakerCafe.com*
*ReallyCheapNames.com*
*CoachingClientForms.com*
*BartsCookbook.com*
*BartsCookies.com*
*TVGuest.com*

# NOTES NOTES NOTES

After reading **99+ *SPEAKER SUCCESS TACTICS***, what stood out for you? What kinds of speaker success tips and actionable items are you going to start implementing right away? Take a few moments to reflect and jot down a few notes that will help you and then make it happen!

_____

_____

_____

_____

_____

_____

_____

_____

_____

_____

# SPEAKER RESOURCES & MORE

# BART'S OTHER BOOKS

If you liked **99+ *SPEAKER SUCCESS TACTICS***, then head on over to **BartSmith.com/books** to check out Bart's other **25+ books** on business, coaching, networking, relationships, and more!

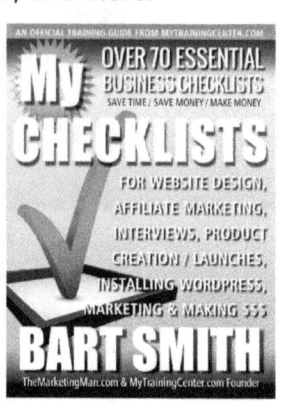

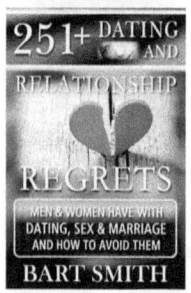

# BART'S TRAINING CENTER

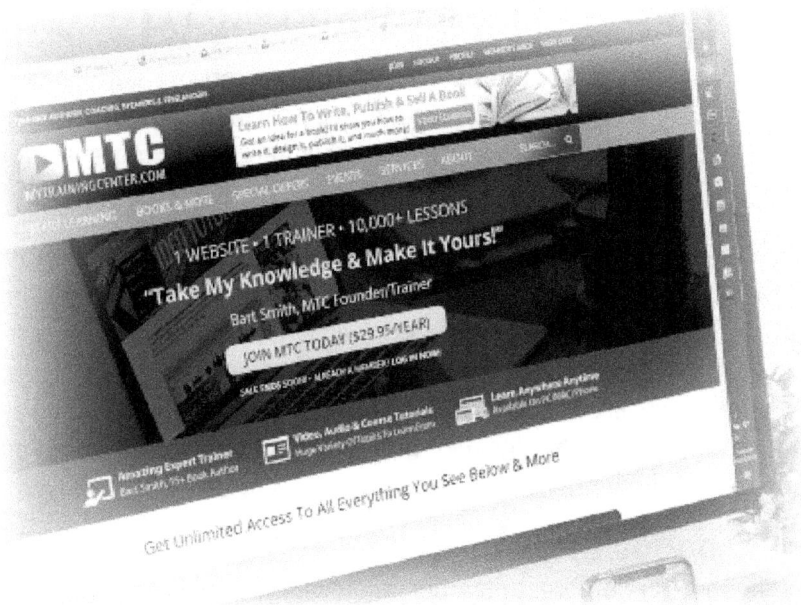

If you like how Bart writes, teaches and shares his knowledge, then head on over to **BartSmith.com/training** and learn more about:

- **How To Write A Book**
- **Audio Recording**
- **Start/Run a Coaching Business**
- **WordPress/Website Design**
- **Membership Websites**
- **Video Recording/Marketing**
- **Graphic Design Skills**
- **Publicity Interviewing**
- **Computer Skills**
- **Networking**
- **Motivation**
- **Marketing/Publicity**

# BartSmith.com/training

ALL LESSONS TAUGHT BY BART: SELF-PUBLISHING, WEBSITE DESIGN, WORDPRESS, PR / PUBLICITY / MARKETING, SPEAKER TRAINING, AUDIO RECORDING, VIDEO MARKETING & SO MUCH MORE!

# SPEAKERCAFE.COM

# DIRECTORY "PROFILE LISTING"

**WHAT IS IT?** Directory profile listings on **SpeakerCafe.com** quickly and publicly showcase your speaker services as the expert to call on to be booked as a speaker for someone's upcoming event or need for a speaker.

**WHY HAVE A PROFILE LISTING ON SPEAKERCAFE.COM?** While most websites get lost like grains of sand on a beach, SpeakerCafe.com profiles stand out to those looking to find speakers for their events. Sure, they could go to your website IF they knew about you. What most event planners like to do is stop by SpeakerCafe.com real quick to see if there's a speaker that fits their needs. If you don't have a listing on SpeakerCafe.com, then you're guaranteed not to be seen or booked.

**WHAT DO YOU GET WITH YOUR SPEAKERCAFE.COM LISTING?** While there are different membership levels you can subscribe to, in general, every member gets to publicly display all of the following to help win the minds of potential TV show personnel decision-makers looking to book TV guests for their TV shows. You get to display:

- ★ Name / Title / Profession
- ★ Contact Info (Phone# / eMail)
- ★ Bio / About / Description
- ★ Post Speaking Topics
- ★ Upload Audio & Video
- ★ Upload Articles & Photos

**SELF-MANAGED SPEAKERCAFE.COM PROFILE LISTINGS:** That's right! You get to create, login and maintain your own profile listing yourself. This is perfect when you want to add more content to your profile listing, such as new videos, photos and articles, update your contact info, etc.

**SpeakerCafe.com PROFILE LISTING COST:** While we are always running specials, if you consider this an investment into making you more money and getting you more exposure, write this off as a tax-deductible advertising expense and get listed today!

## SpeakerCafe.com

# Your Name

Professional Speaker
YourWebsite.com
Your Town, ST 00000

📞 CALL (000) 000-0000

**Contact This Speaker**

**Review This Speaker**

💬 MAKE A CONNECTION! Your Name would like to hear from you. **Contact This Speaker!**

BIO    TOPICS    AUDIENCES    PHOTOS    VIDEOS    TESTIMONIALS

## Contact Information:

| | |
|---|---|
| Website | http://YourWebsite.com |
| Social Profiles | 🇫 🇪 🇮🇳 ▶️ 🇬 🔊 ⬛ Ⓦ |
| Telephone | 000-000-0000 |
| One-Sheet | View My Speaker One-Sheet / Brochure |
| Travels From | Your Town, State |
| Credentials | Enter your credentials, awards, recognition statements, accomplishments, etc., in your field of experience or experience to impress potential companies/organizations looking to book you as a speaker. |

*GET YOUR LISTING TODAY!*

## MEET (YOUR NAME)

### ENTER YOUR SPEAKING TOPICS
that you would like to speak on ...

Write 1-2 paragraphs that describe the problem out in the world and perhaps what's not being done about it. This problem/topic is what you want to be interviewed on because you're the expert that can solve this problem, shed light on it, explain it better, set the record straight, etc.

• List how people are suffering from this problem ...
• What's common among people with this problem ...
• State facts, bullets, and lists of problems

**Again, this is just a sample SpeakerCafe.com DIRECTORY PROFILE LISTING that gives companies the info they need and on ONE PAGE to decide if you're the perfect speaker for their next event! GET YOUR LISTING TODAY!**

# SpeakerCafe.com

# "PROFILE LISTING" CATEGORIES

**These categories represent niche subjects companies and organizations need speakers for.** Peruse these categories. Could you speak effectively on any one (or more) of these topics? If so, get your directory listing today so you can be seen tomorrow by those looking to book speakers for their next event.

ADD & ADHD
Abuse
Accountability
Achievement
Addiction / Recovery
Adoption / Fostering
Adult Entertainment
Adventurers
Advertising
African-American
Aging / Anti-Aging
Alcoholism
American History
American Legends
Anger Management
Animals
Archaeology
Art Performances
Arts & Pop Culture
Athletics / Sports
Attitude
Author
Autism
Awareness & Prevention
Body Language
Branding
Bullying
Business
Business Building
Business Entrepreneurship
Business Growth
Business Trends
Business of Healthcare
Cancer
Cancer Awareness
Career

Celebrity
Celebrity Chefs
Celebrity Speakers
Change
Character Portrayals
China
Christian
Chronic Diseases
Cirque / Acrobats
Coaching
College/University
Comedy
Communication
Communities
Community Relations
Competition
Conflict Resolution
Construction / Building
Consulting
Consumer Trends
Corporate Culture
Corporate Responsibility
Corporate Social Responsibility
Creativity
Crisis
Cultural
Cultural Diversity
Customer Service
Dental Health / Tooth Care
Difficult People
Disability Issues
Disaster Recovery
Domestic Violence
Drug Abuse
Eating Disorders
Ecommerce / Online Sales

Economy
Education
Elementary Education
Emotional Balance
Employees / Workforce
Empowerment
Energy (Oil, Gas, etc.)
Entertainment
Entrepreneurship
Environmental
Environmental Policy
Ethics & Values
Etiquette
Exercise / Fitness
Facilitator
Family
Finance & Insurance
Financial Freedom
Food
Franchising
Freedom
Fundraising
Futurists
Gender Issues
Generation Issues
Global Business
Global Issues
Goal Setting
Government/Politics
Green Issues / Living
Grief
HIV, Aids & STD
Happiness
Health
Health & Beauty
Health & Nutrition

Healthcare Experts
Healthy Lifestyle
History
Home & Garden
Home Health / Care Giving
Homeland Security
Human / Sex Trafficking
Human Resources
Humor
Identity Theft & Safety
Image / Self Esteem
Innovation & Creativity
Inspiration
International Affairs
Internet / World Wide Web
Internet Marketing
Investing / Financial Issues
Judicial System
Language
Law
Law of Attraction
Leadership
Learning Disorders
Life After Work
Life At Work
Life Balance
Lifestyle
Listening Skills
Magic / Illusion
Management
Marketing
Master of Ceremonies
Media
Medical
Men
Mental Health
Mentalists & Hypnotists
Metaphysics
Midlife Transitions
Military
Military / Veterans
Mind / Body Medicine
Money Mindset
Motivation
NLP
Negotiation

Networking
News & Current Events
Nutrition
Olympic Athletes
Organizational Skills
Overcoming Adversity
Parenting & Children
Patriotism
Peak Performance
Performance Improvement
Personal / Life Coaching
Personal Development
Personal Safety
Personality Testing
Pets
Photography
Political
Political Humor
Presentation Skills
Productivity
Profitability
Prosperity
Psychology
Publicity / Public Relations
Real Estate
Reality TV Stars
Recruitment & Retention
Relationships
Religion
Restaurant Industry
Retail
Retirement / Aging
Revues & Variety Shows
Risk Management
Safety
Sales
Science & Engineering
Security
Self Empowerment
Self Help
Self-Publishing
Sex & Sensuality
Sex Education
Sexual Abuse
Small Business
Social Causes

Social Media
Social Services
Spirituality
Sports
Spouse Programs
Strategic Planning
Stress & Anxiety
Success
Succession Planning
Suicide Awareness
Sustainability
TED Conference
TEDX Conference
Tax Planning
Team Building
Technology
Teens
Time Management
Top News
Travel/Tourism
Vaccines
Videography
Vision / Eyesight
Vision / Purpose
Volunteerism
Web Design
Weight Loss
Wellness
Women
Women In Business
Women In Society
Work/Life Balance
Workplace Safety
Writing
Youth Issues

GET YOUR
LISTING
TODAY!

ON
SpeakerCafe.com

# "PROFILE LISTING" CONTENT

What do you get to advertise/showcase publicly in front of hundreds, if not thousands, of potential companies looking to book speakers for their next event? With your **SpeakerCafe.com directory profile listing**, you get to add all of the following to your profile to showcase your speaking talents. For example, you can showcase:

- ☑ YOUR **FULL NAME**
- ☑ YOUR **COMPANY NAME**
- ☑ YOUR **PHONE NUMBER**
- ☑ YOUR **WEBSITE**
- ☑ YOUR **AVAILABILITY**
- ☑ YOUR **SPEAKER FEES**
- ☑ YOUR **CITY/STATE** (LOCATION YOU TRAVEL FROM)
- ☑ YOUR **PHOTO** (PROFESSIONAL HEAD SHOT)
- ☑ YOUR **CREDENTIALS** (EXPERT BIO, DEGREES, ETC.)
- ☑ YOUR **SOCIAL MEDIA ACCOUNTS** (VIA LINKS)
- ☑ **SPEAKING TOPICS/IDEAS** (ONE OR MORE)
- ☑ **SPEAKER TESTIMONIALS** (FROM PAST GIGS)
- ☑ **ARTICLES** (ABOUT YOUR SPEAKING NICHE/TOPICS)
- ☑ **PHOTOS** (SHOWING YOU SPEAKING)
- ☑ **VIDEOS** (SHOWING YOU SPEAKING)
- ☑ **EVENTS** (POST UPCOMING SPEAKING GIGS)

**GET YOUR LISTING TODAY!**

SPEAKERCAFE.COM

Pretty much everything you can add to your profile is speaker-related, speaker-focused, and rich with (your) contact information so event planners know how to contact you immediately and without any middle-man taking a % of any paid speaker profits to possibly book you as a speaker for their upcoming event!

# "PROFILE LISTING" USES

Now that you know what a **SpeakerCafe.com directory profile listing** looks like, the categories you can align yourself with, in addition to the content you can display to help attract potential companies and organizations to book you to speak, the next question is, **what can you do with your SpeakerCafe directory profile listing**? Well, here are all the ways you can use your SpeakerCafe.com directory profile listing:

☑ USE IT TO **PITCH COMPANIES TO BOOK YOU FOR SPEAKING** – It's easy to pitch practically any company to book you if you have all your speaker-related/speaker-focused information in one place, making it easy to find, easy to read/follow and easy to contact you! Why wouldn't you get booked *in a flash* to be someone's next speaker?

☑ USE IT AS **YOUR RESUME** – Looking to get booked from a potential client? Send them to your SpeakerCafe.com directory listing. They can see all your expertise, view your credentials, see sample videos of you speaking, see the topics you speak on, and much more.

☑ USE IT AS **YOUR WEBSITE** – You might like to use your SpeakerCafe.com directory listing profile as your actual website. Why? Because it costs A LOT of money to build and maintain an actual website, let alone TIME to build it. Considering the complexity of maintaining a website today, why bother? Just use your SpeakerCafe directory listing to showcase what you do, link to your social media accounts, attract clients to book you to speak and much more!

GET YOUR **SPEAKERCAFE DIRECTORY PROFILE LISTING** TODAY! GO TO:

# SPEAKERCAFE.COM